Animals Have Feelings, Too!

Exploring Emotions from A to Z

written by
Karen Lee Stevens

illustrated by
Teri Rider

To Miss Bella, who is never afraid to share her feelings, especially at mealtime!
–K.L.S.

...wie, who shared the magical healing power of kitties and always helped me feel good inside and out.
–T.R.

● ● ● ● ●

Published by **All for Animals,**
a nonprofit organization dedicated to creating a compassionate world for animals and children
through humane education and literacy programs that nurture the human-animal bond.

PO Box 3534, Santa Barbara, CA 93130, allforanimals.org

With special thanks to the **Wendy P. McCaw Foundation**
for their support and for sharing our vision of
enhancing the quality of life for both humans and animals.

Animals Have Feelings, Too!
Text copyright © 2011, 2013 by Karen Lee Stevens
Illustrations copyright © 2011, 2013 by Teri Rider
Book design by Teri Rider

All rights reserved. First edition 2011. Second edition 2013.
Printed in the U.S.A.

Library of Congress Control Number: 2011915147
ISBN Number: 978-0-9837625-0-8

00 19 18 17 16 15 14 13   1 2 3 4 5 6 7 8 9

Hi Kids,

My name is Sandy and I'm a yellow Labrador retriever. Most of the time, I'm a happy-go-lucky pup, but once in awhile, I feel lonely or grumpy, too. Just like you, I experience lots of different emotions (that's a BIG word for feelings).

When I'm happy, I wag my tail and let out a soft *ruff-ruff-ruff* as if to say *Let's play!* When I'm annoyed or frightened, I may grumble and growl, meaning *Back off, buddy! Stay away!*

My feline friend, Willow, likes to remind me that I'm not perfect, but I love her anyhow. And that's why I've asked her to help me introduce you to my very favorite feeling words. I hope you'll share them with your human family and, of course, your furry and feathered friends!

Love,
Sandy

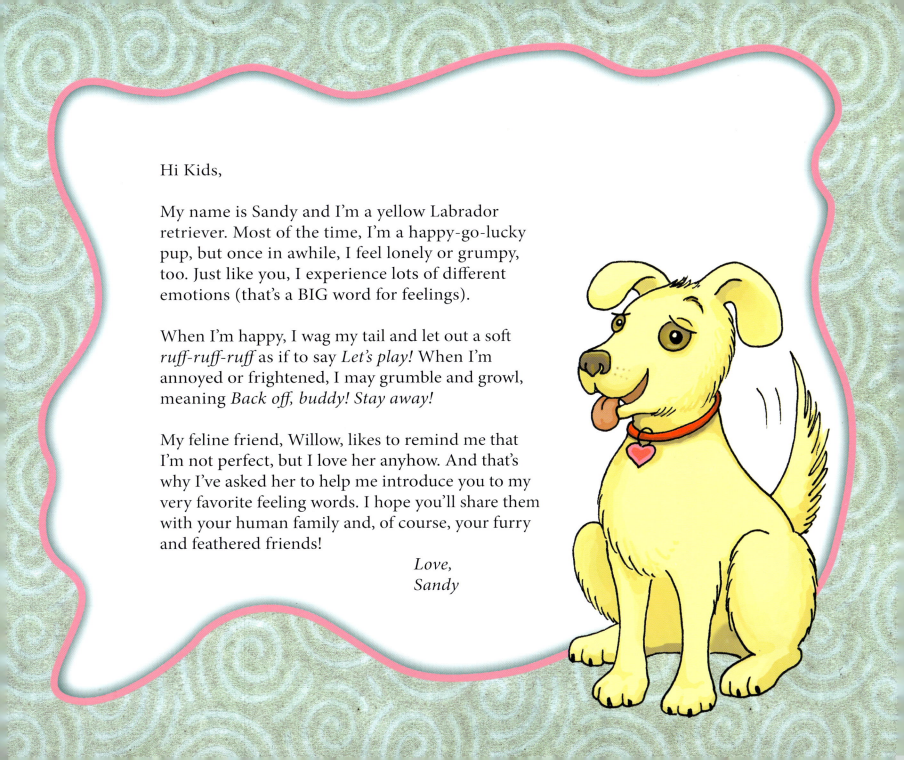

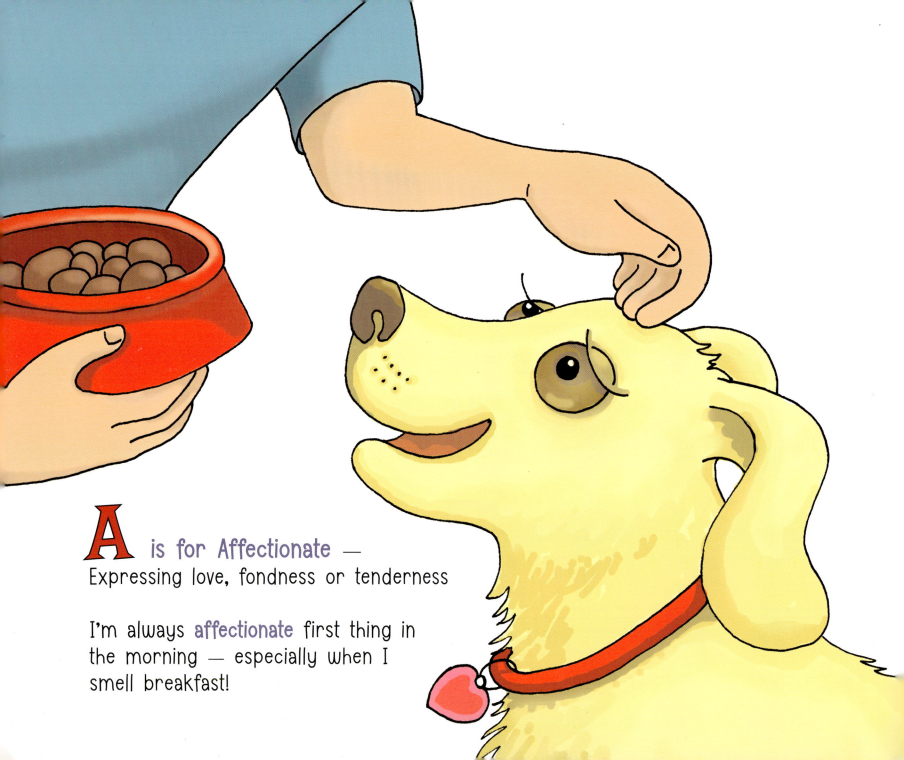

A is for Affectionate —
Expressing love, fondness or tenderness

I'm always **affectionate** first thing in the morning — especially when I smell breakfast!

B is for Bubbly — Lively, excited

Whenever I hear the jingling of my leash, I feel bubbly inside because I know it's time for my walk.

C is for Compassionate — Kind, caring

Being compassionate means you really care about someone's feelings.

D is for Determined — Decided, having reached a decision

I didn't catch the Frisbee on the first try, but I am **determined** to get it this time!

E is for Envious — Jealous

I'm envious because the dog next door has a giant bone as a treat and all I have is this old stick.

F is for Frightened — Afraid, scared

The BOOM! and CRASH! of last night's thunderstorm really frightened Willow and me.

G is for Grumpy — Irritable, grouchy, in a bad mood

You'd be grumpy too if a noisy lawnmower woke you up from a nap!

H is for Heroic — Brave, courageous

The local newspaper called me heroic after I rescued a little girl who had fallen into the deep end of a pool.

I is for Impatient — Anxious, unable to wait

WOOF! WOOF! I'm so impatient to go to the park and my family is taking soooo long to get ready.

J is for Jolly — Happy, joyful

I always have a jolly good time playing with my BFF. (In case you're wondering, BFF means Best Furry Friend!)

K is for Kooky — Unusual, silly, out of the ordinary

People sometimes call me kooky when they see me running in circles. I think it's fun and good exercise, too.

L is for Lonely — Unhappy about being alone

When my family goes to school or work, I feel lonely. It's a good thing that they leave lots of toys for me to play with.

M is for Mischievous — Naughty, ill-behaved
and for Mad — Angry

Stealing Willow's yummy dinner was a mischievous thing to do. Boy, was she mad!

N is for Nauseated — Sick to your stomach

After eating a candy bar, I started feeling nauseated. It tasted so good, but I know chocolate is not good for dogs.

O is for Overjoyed — Delighted, elated, thrilled

I am so overjoyed when my family comes home that I always do a little happy dance.

P is for Perplexed —
Puzzled, bewildered

I'm perplexed when Willow brushes up against my leg. I think it's her way of showing that she likes me.

Q is for Quiet — Silent, shhh...

It's 3 a.m. and my family is sleeping. I must be **quiet** and try not to bark, even though I hear raccoons scurrying on the deck outside.

R is for Relaxed — Free of worry or anxiety

The soft rumbling of Willow's purr helps me feel relaxed.

is for Surprised — Unexpected, astonished

Willow **surprised** me when she sprang out of her favorite hiding place.

T is for Tenderness —
Soft, gentle, delicate

Dogs and cats enjoy being petted with **tenderness**. I LOVE tummy rubs, but most cats like Willow would rather be scratched under the chin.

U is for Uncomfortable —
Painful, irritating

Rolling in the dirt is lots of fun, but getting sticks and leaves stuck in my fur is doggone uncomfortable. It's time for a bath!

V is for Voiceless — Unable to speak

Some people say animals are voiceless. Actually, we have plenty to say! But we express our feelings and needs with barks, meows, squawks and squeaks rather than with words.

W is for Worried — Concerned, anxious, fearful

Although I'm worried by all the strange sounds and smells at the veterinary clinic, I know I'll get a treat after my exam, which always makes me feel better.

X is for XOXO — An expression for hugs and kisses

I'm so excited that you're reading this book!
XOXO,
Sandy

Y is for Youthful — Appearing or feeling young, fresh, vibrant

Even though I'm 10 years old (that's about 70 in people years!), a good diet and lots of exercise helps me stay youthful.

Z is for Zonked — Exhausted, super-duper tired

Guess who is zonked after spending the afternoon chasing tennis balls in the backyard?

Now you know all my favorite feeling words. Remember, just like you, animals have feelings, too!

NOTE TO GROWN-UPS

Animals share many of the same feelings and basic needs that people do. To help your child learn this important concept, here's a fun activity you can do together.

Using crayons or colored pencils, draw several circles on a piece of paper. Under each circle, write a feeling word such as *happy, sad, frightened* or *surprised*. Next, ask your child to draw a facial expression that corresponds with each word. Discuss how animals can feel these emotions as well.

Do you have a favorite feeling word that you'd like to see in our next book? If so, please let us know about it by contacting us at the address below.

• • • • •

All for Animals is a nonprofit organization dedicated to creating a compassionate world for animals and children through humane education and literacy programs that nurture the human-animal bond.

We provide two specially designed programs for young people: *ARF! (Animals + Reading = Fun!)* is an innovative literacy program that gives children an opportunity to improve their reading skills and inspire them to become life-long readers by reading aloud to registered therapy dogs. *Compassion for Critters* is an interactive humane education program that teaches kids to be kind and respectful to animals, people and the environment.

To learn more about the organization or to download a free *Animals Have Feelings, Too!* coloring sheet, please visit allforanimals.org.

All for Animals
PO Box 3534
Santa Barbara, CA 93130
(805) 682-3160
info@allforanimals.org

Photo by Paul Bryant / Left Coast Digital

Karen Lee Stevens is a Certified Humane Education Specialist and the founder and president of All for Animals, a nonprofit, humane education and literacy organization in Santa Barbara, California. From the time she was 4 years old and her mom read *Three Little Kittens* to her, Karen has been fascinated by animals and the written word. This is her first children's book.

Sandy, a yellow Labrador retriever, is a beloved member of the All for Animals' family. After accepting a position as the organization's Canine Ambassador, Sandy began lending a helping paw during classroom visits, enthusiastically introducing herself to children of all ages and happily accepting treats and tummy rubs from kids and adults alike. During her free time, Sandy enjoys chasing tennis balls, camping, backpacking (she has her own backpack!) and lounging under a giant oak tree in her backyard.

Teri Rider is an illustrator and book designer whose love of art is equal to her love of animals and nature. From the time she was a toddler and could hold a pencil, she started drawing animals and eventually found her way into a perfect career illustrating books. Today, Teri lives near San Diego, California and surrounds herself with pets of all kinds, most of them rescues, all with a story. To find out more about Teri, visit her website at teririder.com.